Special Forces Library

ROY FARRAN

Winged Dagger

Adventures on Special Service

GRAFTON BOOKS

A Division of the Collins Publishing Group

LONDON GLASGOW
TORONTO SYDNEY AUCKLAND

Grafton Books
A Division of the Collins Publishing Group
8 Grafton Street, London W1X 3LA

Published by Grafton Books in association with
Arms & Armour Press Ltd 1988

First published in Great Britain by
William Collins Sons Ltd 1948

Copyright © Roy Farran 1948

ISBN 0-586-20085-1

Printed and bound in Great Britain by
Collins, Glasgow

Set in Times

*None of the characters in this book is fictitious, but some,
for obvious reasons, are not bearing their own names.*